THE

COLLECTION

SAUCY POSTCARDS

MARCUS HEARN

CONSTABLE

For Jonathan and Claire

CONSTABLE

First published in Great Britain in 2013 by Constable, an imprint of Constable & Robinson Ltd.

Copyright © Bamforth & Company Ltd, 2013
Licensed by JELC Ltd

www.bamforthpostcards.co.uk

Text copyright © Marcus Hearn, 2013

Designed by Peri Godbold/Flashpoint

7 9 10 8

A CIP catalogue record for this book
is available from the British Library.

ISBN: 978-1-4721-0546-2

Printed and bound in the EU

Constable
An imprint of
Little, Brown Book Group
Carmelite House
50 Victoria Embankment
London EC4Y 0DZ

An Hachette UK Company
www.hachette.co.uk

www.littlebrown.co.uk

CONTENTS

INTRODUCTION

Right: Early 1950s' artwork by Bamforth's Douglas Tempest, typifying the seaside tradition of saucy postcards.

Below: Even postcards created purely for advertising purposes were vetted for decency. This one was approved by the Isle of Man Postcard Censorship Committee in 1949.

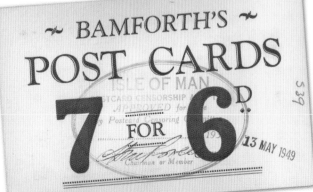

The tradition of saucy postcards is central to British popular culture of the last century. Randy nurses, henpecked husbands and nagging wives were all part of the postcard artists' repertoire long before the *Carry On* films began. Such archetypes were brought to exaggerated life with suggestive jokes and lurid illustrations that are synonymous with the seaside resorts where they were sold.

"I think these cards represent two weeks of the year when people went on holiday to

Bamforth's funniest cards and reveals the background to their publication.

The story begins in Holmfirth, a small town six miles south of Huddersfield in West Yorkshire. Holmfirth is best remembered as the picturesque location for the BBC sitcom *Last of the Summer Wine*, but the town had a comic claim to fame long before that programme started production in 1972.

The original Bamforth company was a photography business established at Holmfirth's Station Road in 1870. Thirteen years later the founder, James Bamforth (born 1842), diversified into the production of magic lantern slides based on his own pictures. The Station Road premises became a factory with a photographic studio on the

Fat ladies were a favourite theme of Bamforth's seaside designs for decades. The card below reproduces Sandy Powell's 1930s' radio catchphrase, "Can you hear me, Mother?" The above two examples date from 1963.

MOTHER'S BEHIND AGAIN

a different place that had different rules," says Dr Nick Hiley, head of the British Cartoon Archive. "That holiday promised all sorts of things – more and better food, more drink, more sun and more sex. And it promised more self expression and freedom. The cards help to define that whole liberty."

Arguably the most successful publisher of such postcards is Bamforth & Co, a company that thrived for well over 100 years. This book presents a selection of

Right: The exterior of Bamforth's premises at 12 Station Road, Holmfirth, in 1903.

Far right: James Bamforth, the photographer who started the Bamforth company in 1870.

Below: The photography for postcards and magic lantern slides took place in the top floor studio at Station Road.

top floor. The Victorians' fascination with this early form of mass entertainment led to increasingly sophisticated projectors becoming available by the 1880s. Bamforth responded with a wide variety of hand-coloured photographic slides that proved so popular that in 1898 an extension was built to the Station Road factory to facilitate increased output. An estimated 1,400 sets of slides, comprising 20,000 images, were made available between 1883 and the

beginning of the First World War. Bamforth advertising declared the company to be 'The Largest Producer in the World', although contemporary descriptions of the studio suggest a cottage industry frugality. "He chose homely themes, due to his use of neighbours as models and sitters," said the February 1899 issue of *Photogram* magazine. "Thus it came about, to his lasting credit, that the simple characters of his stories combined with the naturalness of the leading figures in them, has endeared his life model sets to millions of children and adults."

James understood his market – many of the life model sets were presented in religious narratives for projection at Sunday Schools, or with a moralistic message that was ideal for Temperance Society lectures. Newspapers dubbed him 'King of the Lantern Slides' and by the end of the 19th century the company was best known for its 'Illustrated Song Series'. The 1912

set commemorating the sinking of the *Titanic* presented the unfolding tragedy in a vividly coloured series of photographs and illustrations. These included images of the ship striking the iceberg, passengers clambering aboard lifeboats, a radio operator frantically signalling for help and the captain, Edward Smith, with waves lapping around his knees. During screenings of the slides audiences were encouraged to sing 'Be British', the song composed as part of the huge charity drive to help families of the deceased.

With a studio, his own painted backcloths and a repertory company of local models prepared to sit for little or no money, it is perhaps unsurprising that James took a keen interest in the burgeoning art of filmmaking. In 1896 Bradford's Riley Brothers commissioned Bamforth to make films with the initial aim of demonstrating their newly bought kinematograph camera for customers. James' son Frank (born 1872)

Above: A selection of hand-coloured magic lantern slides produced by Bamforth. From left to right, slides from: *Mary Stubbs' Dream: or, Christmas Eve at the Blue Boar* (1897), *Harry's Pint, or Threepence a Day* (1898) and *The Lifeboat* (1899). The latter two feature James Bamforth in key roles.

would act as director, his daughter 'Miss Jane' (born 1878) became an all-round production assistant and another son Edwin (born 1877) had small acting roles. James' oldest son Harry (born 1867) projected the films in public halls, using a phonograph to provide a musical soundtrack. At least 15 'RAB' films were produced by James

Right: Edwin Bamforth became the managing director of the company following the death of his father, James. Edwin was the first to realise the potential in selling artist-drawn comic postcards at seaside resorts.

between 1898 and 1900. "My grandfather was a genius," recalled Derek Bamforth in 2006. "Not only was he a great artist, he was a great entrepreneur and to have that history in the family is wonderful."

James Bamforth had few contemporaries among British filmmakers at the turn of the century, but aside from pioneering camera techniques he can also be credited with the introduction of slapstick humour familiar from the northern music halls. Working alongside Frank and Edwin, James would sometimes take magic lantern slides as inspiration for his silent films. The comic short *Women's Rights* was based on a set of slides in which a Suffragette and her friend were humiliated by 'Mr Niggle' and his son.

Women's Rights was filmed in 1899, two years after the Women's Suffrage Bill was defeated in parliament and four years before the Pankhursts founded the Women's Social and Political Union. The film's fledgling Suffragettes are two ladies (both played by men) who are first seen standing by a fence in a field. A couple of lads creep up to the other side of the fence and surreptitiously nail their skirts to it. When the two ladies discover

their predicament they attempt to beat the flat-capped pranksters with their parasols but end up running on the spot.

Kiss in the Tunnel, a more sophisticated RAB production from 1899, was made with co-operation from the local railway. "If they needed a train shot the station master would signal the driver to bring the train in slowly," Derek Bamforth told *The Sunday Express* in 2006. "But if my grandfather missed the take they would just send it back out again and do it until it was absolutely right. Of course, it was a regular train full of fee-paying passengers and goodness knows how delayed they were by the time filming had finished – but no one seemed to mind."

Like *Women's Rights, Kiss in the Tunnel* runs to little over a minute but employs the continuity editing of three different shots in a surprisingly casual depiction of young romance. The first shot shows a steam train heading into a tunnel. We then cut to a couple alone in a carriage. The man strikes a match on the underside of his boot and lights a cigarette. He then rests the cigarette on the edge of the window and crosses to the opposite seat, where his demure companion has been hiding her face behind a magazine.

She immediately puts the magazine aside and in the darkness of the tunnel they kiss. We then cut to the train pulling into a station.

This was essentially a three-shot remake of a film with the same title produced by George Albert Smith earlier the same year, but aside from its sophisticated editing the new version featured a rather more passionate kiss.

Although Edwin would resume filmmaking on a grander scale from 1913 to 1915, the Bamforths' original flirtation with cinema was relatively brief. "I think they probably believed that films were just a passing phase and that they'd never get seriously rich from it," said Derek.

James was soon diverted by another enterprise – the production of picture postcards. The General Post Office had been issuing postcards in Great Britain since 1870 – coincidentally the year that James founded his photographic studio – and in 1894 the Royal Mail granted publishers permission to design and sell picture postcards. In 1902 the government allowed an adaptation of the standard postcard design, dividing the back of a card into two halves – one for the

Above: Three shots were edited together in Bamforth's pioneering and distinctly saucy film *Kiss in the Tunnel* (1899).

message and one for the address. The fronts of cards could now be wholly pictorial, and this led to a boom in collecting and correspondence. Bamforth began publishing picture postcards in 1903, with many of the earliest designs derived from their extensive library of magic lantern slides. By 1908 approximately 860 million cards were being posted in Great Britain every year. As well as the lantern slide designs, Bamforth's range included scenes with sentimental messages and cards bearing the lyrics of popular songs and hymns.

Around 1906 Harry Bamforth emigrated to the United States to manage the company's New York office, and in June 1910 Bamforth became a limited company, with James, Edwin and Frank as the directors. James died in 1911, by which time future managing director Edwin had seen the potential in producing a series of artist-drawn comic postcards aimed at holiday makers in seaside resorts. Following the tradition of *Women's Rights* and *Kiss in the Tunnel*, from here on Bamforth's picture postcards would enter more risqué territory. After 1918 the popularity of sentimental

Right: Douglas Tempest and his daughter Margaret, pictured in 1933.

Far right: Margaret was the model for this cheeky Bamforth postcard.

Will this satisfy you if 4 can get it home?

postcards sharply declined, making way for the comic postcards that would eventually define Bamforth & Co.

The creation of a distinctive style for Bamforth's comic postcards was largely down to the company's first staff artist. Douglas Tempest was born in 1887 and trained at the Leeds School of Art before he joined Bamforth in 1912. He ultimately became a director of the company, staying until his death in 1954. Although not as well-known as the notorious Donald McGill (whose work Bamforth distributed in America), Tempest made a comparable contribution to the art of the comic postcard. It is estimated that he produced up to 10,000 sketches for Bamforth, and the popularity of his designs helped initiate the company's shift away from using photographic models.

Tempest remained Bamforth's only staff artist throughout the First World War, and while a heart condition prevented him from serving he made his contribution to the war effort with numerous morale-boosting cards mocking Kaiser Wilhelm II and his hapless soldiers. The saucy postcards continued through the war years, and while these seem quaint compared to the bawdy jokes and illustrations that followed, many were considered racy at the time.

Above: A selection of Tempest comic postcards published between 1916 and 1918.

A little bit of green at Xmas is pleasing to the eye

"HERE'S ONE FOR YOU—AND ONE FOR THE MISSUS—CHEERIO!"

A "BAMFORTH" COMIC

"I'M GOING TO HAVE PNEUMONIA, LASS!"
"YER HAVING **NOWT** TILL I'VE HAD A NEW HAT!"

A BAMFORTH COMIC

Clockwise from top: This 1914 design was one of Bamforth's earliest saucy postcards; a 1953 example of sponsored advertising on a Bamforth card; Arnold Taylor's first illustration for the company; a highlight of Philip W Taylor's work.

Arnold Taylor (born 1910) joined the Bamforth staff in 1926, training under Tempest as his apprentice. He left the company to serve in the Second World War, sustained an injury in Egypt during the Western Desert Campaign, and returned to civilian life as a freelance illustrator. He was persuaded to return to Bamforth as a full-time artist and, like Tempest, was offered a directorship. Over the course of more than 60 years Taylor produced an astonishing number of illustrations for Bamforth, and it is his work that dominates this book.

The third of Bamforth's staff artists was Philip W Taylor (no relation to Arnold), who was 16 when he joined the company in 1937.

In 1996 he shared his memories of his fellow artists with Peter Tucker of *Picture Postcard Monthly*. Philip remembered Tempest as "a most agreeable man. He, his wife and daughter Margaret lived within walking distance of the warehouse. He wore bow ties and showed me how to tie one."

"IS THAT YOUR DOG, MISS?"
"OF COURSE IT IS!"
"WELL, YOU CAN PULL THE CHAIN, **HE'S FINISHED!**"

A "BAMFORTH" COMIC

Philip recalled that before the war Arnold was "unmarried and an extremely fit young man. He rode a Panther motorbike very fast, bent six inch nails with his bare hands, and tossed 56 pound weights around during the lunch break... [Arnold] never made me feel like a kid. He was always ready to show me how to improve my work, which made the transition from school to the workplace exciting as well as pleasant."

After the Second World War Philip Taylor emigrated to New Zealand but continued to make contributions to Bamforth's range of folded greetings cards.

Bamforth only ever employed four staff artists, and the last of these joined the company from the Barnsley School of Art in 1955. Brian Fitzpatrick (born 1932) trained under Arnold Taylor, who remembered his apprentice as "a very forthright person" who was unafraid to challenge the taboos of the day. "Between us, we produce 78 comic cards each year," Taylor told Ralph Jones in 1964. "First we think up the jokes and make

pencil roughs, about 200 of them. From these 200 roughs, 78 are chosen. The choice is made by Mr Bamforth, myself, Brian Fitzpatrick and the two representatives who have to eventually sell the cards... One has to keep up with modern trends and ideas, to be topical and 'with it', and it is of course a very difficult business getting ideas for comic cards year after year. I sometimes wonder where the ideas are coming from for the next edition but somehow they keep coming."

The "Mr Bamforth" Taylor referred to was John Derek (born 1919), who was still a teenager when he became managing director of the family firm in 1938. After the war Derek returned to Bamforth & Co to oversee a period of expansion into greetings cards and calendars, as well as the comic postcards and scenic views that remained the core of the business.

Below: Brian Fitzpatrick's first Bamforth card.

Bottom: Original artwork for Fitzpatrick's hotel roof postcard, published in 1962. The gag was recycled with new artwork in 1971.

Opposite: Arnold Taylor (standing) and Brian Fitzpatrick at work in the Bamforth studio on 31 October 1961.

The production process was illustrated in *The Brook*, a corporate film commissioned by the Huddersfield company Brook Electric Motors in 1960. A large part of the film is devoted to Brook's plant, but neighbouring businesses such as Bamforth & Co are also featured. We see Derek Bamforth surrounded by Arnold Taylor, Brian Fitzpatrick and two sales reps. "This is the group of people who select the cartoons for most of the seaside comics we buy every year," says the narrator. The finished artwork is shown being pasted onto boards, nine at a time, for the preparation of printing blocks. The proofs are approved by Taylor and Fitzpatrick and we cut to the downstairs part of the Bamforth factory, where "the girls take over to sort and dispatch the cards to the seaside resorts."

The passage from drawing board to shop counter was not always smooth. Along with rock and roll, Hammer horror and commercial television, saucy postcards were considered a threat to the moral fabric of post-war Britain. In 1941 George Orwell had recoiled from the "overpowering vulgarity" and "ever-present

obscenity" of comic postcards in his essay about Donald McGill, before concluding that "The corner of the human heart they speak for might easily manifest itself in worse forms, and I for one should be sorry to see them vanish."

Sir Theobald Mathew, the Director of Public Prosecutions from 1944 to 1964, took a less sentimental view. In 1950 Derek Bamforth visited the Chief Constable of Blackpool in an effort to find out more about the campaign that had recently resulted in 14 local traders being fined for displaying 'obscene' postcards. The repeated confiscation and destruction of such stock could have disastrous consequences for business, and Derek was mindful of retailers' increasing disillusionment.

He believed the solution lay in formal postcard censorship. In much the same way that the film industry's compliance with the British Board of Film Censors pre-empted state-imposed regulation, it was felt that if publishers complied with the judgements of postcard censorship committees then the police and the DPP would have less justification for pursuing their own agenda. On 6 November Derek told *The Daily Mirror*, "There is an awful lot of filth on the market. Holidaymakers need something broad, but not as broad as the openly sexy double-meaning cards that are being sold. We feel retailers must have some guidance. A national censorship board would prevent traders being in danger of a fine for selling cards they probably haven't seen."

Below: Scenes from *The Brook*, the 1960 film showing how Bamforth created and distributed postcards.

"I AINT GOT A VERY LONG FURLOUGH, LIZ!"
"AW, NEVER MIND THAT—YOU CAN WEAR AN OVERCOAT!"

Above: One of the first cards disapproved by the Blackpool Postcard Censorship Board.

Below: Douglas Tempest is approved by the Cleethorpes Comic Card Censorship Committee in 1954.

His ambition for a national organisation was never realised, and in 1951 another 17 shop owners were prosecuted in Blackpool. In an interview with *The Daily Mirror* that year, Blackpool's Police Superintendent Warren revealed the latest methods of detecting and eradicating postcard smut. "Upon receiving a complaint from a member of the public, a plain clothes man is sent to buy a copy of the offending card. When the stationer says

that he can see nothing wrong in the card, he is asked: 'Would you send that card to your daughter?' If the answer is 'No' – as it usually is – a prosecution may follow and other retailers promptly withdraw the same card from their stocks."

Something had to be done to reassure the police, retailers and publishers, so in November Blackpool hosted the first meeting of its local postcard censorship board. The nine-strong group gathered in a club near the rain-swept North Pier, while curious members of the press waited outside. The board included 50-year-old grandmother Gloria Swanson, who shared her name with a Hollywood star but was president elect of the local Hotel and Boarding House Association. The former governess took a stern view of the material. "I can always see the funny side of things, but I don't like blueness," she told *The Daily Mirror*'s Eve Chapman. "Arthur Askey, now, is a clean and entertaining comedian. These

"WHAT'S WRONG WITH YOU?"
"CONSTIPATION, SIR!"
"WHAT DID YOU DO IN CIVILIAN LIFE?"
"VERY SELDOM ANYTHING, SIR, IT'S BEEN MY TROUBLE ALL ALONG!"

"QUICK, DOCTOR, HIS EYES ARE POPPING OUT AND HE'S
CHOKING—SHALL I LOOSEN HIS COLLAR?"
"NO, MISS—**JUST FASTEN YOURS UP!**"

Left: A classic Arnold Taylor illustration and its corresponding postcard. Magistrates in Broadstairs prosecuted a retailer for selling this design in September 1953.

Below: Another risqué gag in sketch form.

dirty postcards with a double meaning should be kept away from children."

Gloria's fellow board members included middle-aged bank manager Frank Holland ("I'm an ordinary businessman with a broad sense of humour doing my duty to the

Right: Arnold Taylor's original illustration makes it clear that he was promoting his employers on the side of the bus. Ryde Magistrates' Court prosecuted a retailer for selling this card in October 1953.

"HOW FAR CAN WE GO FOR THREE BOB, DRIVER?"
"YOU'D BETTER GET IN THE BACK SEAT LADDIE, AND FIND OUT!"

public"), solicitor Basil Woosnam ("I find political cartoons and *Punch* very humorous"), the Reverend CN Wardle-Harpur and Denise Gillet, who bought the stock of cards for her family's two stationers' shops. Also on the board was local shopkeeper Edward Silcock. "It's a tricky business, all right," he told the incredulous Chapman. "I know one man who was in court for selling what seemed a clean card – yet I've seen a right dirty one displayed in a shop for months and the police never bothered about it."

The board's secretary was commercial traveller Thomas Twigg. His explanation of the system did little to reassure those who were hoping that censorship would provide a clear way forward. "We can't prevent retailers from buying these cards from the manufacturers," he said, "but if they are later prosecuted by the police, it won't be our responsibility."

After the meeting the chairman, George Allen, told Chapman: "We had a very enjoyable and successful evening. The 2,000 cards submitted were only the first few of next season's designs, and we seriously considered 400 of them. Most were inoffensive, but 40 were returned to one maker with 'Rejected' stamped on the back in red, and copies of the rejected cards will be sent to the police."

Despite the evident confusion surrounding their activities, the Blackpool Postcard Censorship Board assumed at least nominal responsibility for the estimated 10 million comic postcards that were sold in the town every summer. This was Bamforth's biggest single market, and for that reason if no other they would maintain close links with the board for the next two decades.

Canon Neil Pritchard joined the Blackpool Postcard Censorship Board in 1959 and stayed until 1965. "We were not at all a solemn lot," he told *The Independent*'s John Windsor in January 1994. "We had lots of fun. We even laughed at the designs we disapproved – and the two ladies on the committee (a housewife and a councillor) laughed louder than the men... Even the ladies would not have objected to a design because it was sexist. We banned designs only if we thought they verged on pornography."

Winston Churchill had returned to power just weeks before the first meeting of the Blackpool board. The election of his Conservative government coincided with a rapid escalation of prosecutions under the Obscene Publications Act of 1857. Initially it was just postcard retailers that were targeted by the police. On the orders of local magistrates an estimated 11,662 seaside cards were destroyed in 1951. The following year that number rose to 16,029, before the campaign peaked with the destruction of 32,603 cards in 1953.

Nick Hiley considers that there are several possible sources for this vendetta. "One of the questions that puzzles me is

whether it was maintained by a Conservative government wanting a clean up campaign, getting the Director of Public Prosecutions to orchestrate police raids, or whether it was a reaction to feelings in seaside resorts that these cards had gone too far. Maybe these cards were scaring off the family trade that they wanted?"

As the 1950s continued the postcard censorship committees in Blackpool, Cleethorpes, Great Yarmouth, Hastings

"I DREAMT LAST NIGHT—I WAS CHASING MARILYN MONROE—IT WAS AWFUL!"
"AWFUL, OLD MAN?"
"I'LL SAY IT WAS—SHE GOT AWAY!"

Above: Banned by the Isle of Man in September 1954.

Below: Prosecuted in Ryde, October 1953.

"THE **WIND** SEEMS TO BE BOTHERING YOU, AUNTIE!"
"IT IS LAD, BUT I DIDN'T THINK YOU'D NOTICE IN THIS NOISY MACHINE!"

"TAKE A CHANCE GUV'NOR, BUY IT!— LIFE'S FULL OF SURPRISES!"

BARGAIN £10

A "BAMFORTH" COMIC

DISAPPROVED 1954.

I must say "You've got a COLD NOSE – MISTER JONES!"

Above: This card was prosecuted in Grimsby in November 1953, yet widely distributed outside Lincolnshire.

Far right: The Blackpool Postcard Censorship Board banned this sketch from going any further in August 1957.

and the Isle of Man continued to act independently of each other with predictable consequences. A card prohibited in Hastings could be approved in Great Yarmouth, and vice versa. Not every town had a censorship committee, and even those that did couldn't guarantee retailers immunity from police raids.

"Strangely, the random nature of it made it a much more powerful censorship campaign," says Hiley. "It made retailers more reluctant to stock *anything* suggestive because they just couldn't tell what would be found offensive."

The DPP maintained an index of local prosecutions, with the aim of establishing national guidelines for dealing with obscene postcards. The DPP's records are preserved by the British Cartoon Archive at the University of Kent and make for bewildering reading. The biggest purge began in September 1953, when Lincolnshire police raided 16 shops in Cleethorpes, seizing and

subsequently destroying 5,405 postcards. In the Isle of Wight a few weeks later five shops in Ryde were relieved of more than 5,000 postcards. These too were burned.

The cards seized from Cleethorpes were taken to the magistrates' court in Grimsby, where the police pointed out that the haul included designs that had been confiscated in previous raids. Their actions had failed to deter retailers, so they asked for permission to go after the publishers instead.

The result was the notorious obscenity trial held at Lincoln Crown Court on 15 July the following year. Bamforth & Co were among the eight publishers accused of contravening the Obscene Publications Act, and one of four that ultimately stood trial. Derek Bamforth was appalled at the charge, maintaining that while some of his company's cards were certainly vulgar, none were obscene. His support of the Blackpool Postcard Censorship Board and his service to the Postcard Publishers' Association held him in good stead. Derek and his fellow directors were acquitted, but Donald McGill (a director of publisher D Constance) was not so lucky. The defence counsel's argument that "Some of these [cards], I suggest, are of the traditional English music hall vulgarity which has stood the test of many years" was regarded with cynicism by some quarters of the court, and McGill decided to plead guilty. D Constance and its directors were fined and ordered to pay costs.

Unlike some smaller publishers, Bamforth & Co escaped the Lincoln obscenity trial with their reputation, and their business, intact. Retailers of their cards would, however, continue to be hauled before magistrates' courts for the next seven years. Between 1952 and 1961 cards illustrated by

all four of Bamforth's artists would be the subject of 159 prosecutions, mostly for jokes that now seem utterly innocuous.

A defiant McGill offered to give evidence to the Select Committee considering a bill to amend the Obscene Publications Act, but it appears that the revision was legislated in 1959 without his input. In November the following year Sir Theobald Mathew suffered his most conspicuous setback when Penguin Books were found not guilty for publishing *Lady Chatterley's Lover*. Future obscenity convictions would be harder to secure, and

Below: Racy literature was the subject of this postcard, published in 1947. The sketch alongside was approved in Blackpool in 1961, eight months after the *Chatterley* verdict.

MY GRANDSON'S VERY ADVANCED FOR HIS YEARS, HE'S READING A BOOK CALLED **NO ORCHIDS FOR MISS BLANDISH.** AND LAST WEEK HE READ **FOREVER AMBER !**

A "BAMFORTH" COMIC

"GEE WHIZ DARLING – THIS IS AN **EXCITING BOOK** AND NOT HALF !"

"I BET YOU THINK THAT OLD TIN BATH HAS A BOTTOM IN IT, DON'T YOU LOVE?"

BATHING ALLOWED

A 'BAMFORTH' COMIC

NUDIST CAMP

Above: Prudish magistrates in Brighton objected to this card in November 1961.

Right: Arnold Taylor's artwork for a similarly themed card published in 1960. The caption read: "I can't pick your ball up girls, I've got a bad back – you'll have to nip over and fetch it!"

from that point on there was an apparent reluctance to pursue postcard retailers. The DPP's card index came to an end in 1962, and poet Philip Larkin famously recorded that sexual intercourse began in 1963: "Between the end of the 'Chatterley' ban and the Beatles' first LP."

In this new era of relatively free expression Bamforth's postcards became increasingly explicit. It's probably no coincidence that the popularity of its saucy jokes declined from 1964 onwards. Although censorship committees would become increasingly redundant, Bamforth continued to submit sketches and artwork, burying or delaying designs that were rejected.

The Blackpool committee closed in 1968, shortly after a newsagent in Aberystwyth made a mockery of the whole process by advertising 'Postcards banned by Blackpool Censorship Board'. The Isle of Man committee proved the most durable

and commemorated its demise in 1985 by issuing its own saucy postcard.

"From one point of view, the classic seaside postcards are produced under censorship, because during that time the artists had to walk a tightrope between innocence and obscenity," says Nick Hiley. "The strategy they used to include the obscenity without risk of prosecution was very attractive. The fact that the obscenity bursts out from beneath the innocent exterior of the card still appeals to people. It seems to me that after the end of censorship there is a lot more explicit artwork, and a lot more explicit captions. The obscenity is no longer in the

conjunction between the two. In the earlier cards the vulgarity was created in the mind of the viewer, but by the 1960s and 70s there was vulgarity in the images and the captions."

Fortunately, cards that were rejected by British censorship committees could be exported to other countries. By the early 1960s Bamforth was selling cards in Australia and South Africa, and translating jokes for the French, Dutch and Belgian markets. Many more territories were reached by its foreign agents.

In 1970 Derek Bamforth celebrated his company's centenary by taking his staff

Far left: Taylor's illustration for a card published in 1970. This is an early example of a speech balloon appearing as an integrated part of the original artwork.

Above: The Blackpool Postcard Censorship Board disapproved these dumplings in July 1966.

Left: An export card published in 1965. The caption is presented in French, English and Dutch.

THE MAN WHO INVENTED
THE BIRTH PILL
SHOULD BE AWARDED

FOR
INVENTING
THE
PILL

THE NoBELLIE PRIZE!

POST CARD

ISLE OF MAN.
POSTCARD CENSORSHIP ACT, 1933.
DISAPPROVED for Sale
by Postcard Censoring Committee.

30 DEC 1968 19
.... Chairman or
Member

PLEASE
DO NOT CLEAN
MUDDY BALLS
IN WASH BASIN

Above: Contraception was no joke in the Isle of Man in 1968.

Above right: Charles Grigg's first card for Bamforth, published in 1975.

on a lavish holiday to Amsterdam. In an age where innuendo was becoming passé, Bamforth & Co remained the world's biggest publisher of comic postcards by giving the customers what they wanted. "The appeal of the comic card is its directness and simple vulgarity," Arnold Taylor told *The Daily Mirror*'s Donald Walker in August 1971. "The permissive society has had its effect on what is accepted today. For example, we can now draw nipples on the breasts of cartoon women – something we couldn't have got away with even 18 months ago. We used to send all our cards to a committee of seven in Blackpool. They included lay readers and council officials, and we only used the cards they approved. But we don't bother now. I think we'd have gone out of business if we still listened to them."

As well as the new liberalism, the company faced a more serious challenge in 1974 when Brian Fitzpatrick died of leukaemia, aged just 42. Arnold Taylor

continued as Bamforth's sole staff artist, and from 1975 the list was supplemented by freelancers. The first of these was *Dandy* comic artist Charles 'Chas' Grigg who, working from his home in the West Midlands, contributed more than 170 designs between 1975 and 1991.

In November 1975 there was a threatened return to the bad old days when Blackpool shop owner Mary Baker was prosecuted for "exposing cards of an offensive nature". The cards in question were both published by Bamforth: "Crushed nuts, Grandad?" (reproduced on page 79) and "Have you got cotton wool balls?" Her solicitor argued that public taste had changed drastically, and illustrated his point by showing magistrates pornographic magazines featuring full-frontal naked women *and* men. Mrs Baker pleaded not guilty. The magistrates agreed and made the police pay her £50 costs. In Blackpool at least, the sham of postcard censorship was finally over.

In August 1979, *The Daily Mirror*'s Paul Callan visited the Holmfirth factory and was

amused to discover that the older employees referred to their managing director as "Young Mr Derek". The Bamforth boss was happy to describe his company's postcards as "wonderfully vulgar. Anything subtle just wouldn't sell. We've discovered these things simply by trial and error over the years... We use freelance artists but they often go too far. Many appear to be obsessed with religion and their ideas have to be rejected. We just can't have cards about vicars, priests – and certainly not rabbis. Imagine the trouble we'd be in."

Despite self-censorship, the spectre of political correctness was looming on the horizon. In 1979 Bamforth & Co were reported to the Race Relations Board by an economics lecturer from the New University of Ulster. "It's a 30-year-old joke about an Irishman," said Derek. "Obviously the chap has no sense of humour."

The same could not be said for Derek, who presided over a happy workplace that included seven staff-members with more than 50 years' service. He was a familiar presence in every part of the business, from the boardroom to the dispatch department, and led his staff on the annual works' outings. An era came to an end when both he and Arnold Taylor retired in 1987.

Derek sold the company to the Scarborough-based publisher and printer ETW Dennis & Sons on the proviso that the Bamforth & Co name be preserved, along with continuity of employment for certain staff. In 1994 Dennis moved the Bamforth operation to Scarborough, leaving the Station Road premises to be redeveloped

Above left: One of the cards that landed Mrs Baker in court in 1975.

Above: This 1974 design had become one of Bamforth's biggest sellers by the end of the decade.

Above: Derek Bamforth outside the company's factory in Station Road, Holmfirth.

Above right: Derek was reportedly dismayed by the sale of the Bamforth archive in 1994.

as housing. Dennis' Bamforth-branded comic postcards continued with freelancers Brian Perry and Syd Kitching, artists who maintained the spirit of the series but adopted a distinctively modern style of illustration.

Dennis had already made the controversial decision to sell Bamforth's archive of original artwork, and on 17 February 1994 a widely publicised auction at Christie's raised £88,033. "It does seem a pity," reflected Taylor. "You put all this work in, and then somebody else capitalises on it."

In June 2000 Dennis went into receivership with debts of more than £1 million, but it was the better-known subsidiary Bamforth that attracted most of the unwelcome publicity. In September creditors learned that there was no interest in the parent company, but that several potential buyers had made enquiries about Bamforth. The lucky bidder was Ian Wallace, the Huddersfield-born investor who had opened Liverpool's Beatles Shop in 1982. A comic postcard publisher might have seemed a strange purchase for someone with a background in record retail and an ongoing transport business, but Wallace had fond memories of the cards from his youth. He was hooked as soon as he rifled through the 20-30 boxes that now constituted the Bamforth archive. "I was there for several days in the end," he says. "The images were fantastic, reminding me of Benny Hill and the *Carry On* movies."

Wallace came up with a plan to give Bamforth & Co new life in the 21st century. "I realised, of course, that people don't send postcards in the numbers they used to," he says. "I also realised that it would be very difficult to create new cards that would match the quality of those created by Taylor and Fitzpatrick. However I knew that people recalled these illustrations with great fondness, and even young people liked them. I thought they had potential if they were taken off the postcards and added to other products – everything from beach towels to mouse mats. In short, I recognised that the best of these images weren't old, they were vintage."

In 2001 Wallace attended a convention held by Bamforth enthusiasts. While there, he was happy to reassure Derek Bamforth that the company was in safe hands. Since then, Wallace has continued his efforts to re-assemble a complete archive of Bamforth postcards, navigating the company's incomplete and Byzantine records with the help of collectors and experts such as Dr Nick Hiley.

Derek Bamforth died in 2010. His obituary in *The Huddersfield Daily*

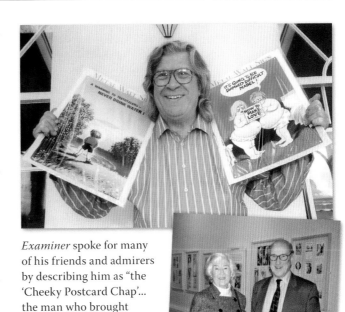

Examiner spoke for many of his friends and admirers by describing him as "the 'Cheeky Postcard Chap'... the man who brought smiles to millions of faces."

Bamforth and Co continue to celebrate his family's legacy. "They were innovators," says Wallace. "They went from producing photographs to magic lantern slides, films and then postcards. They didn't stand still, and it's important that we're just as adaptable. The best of the artwork will endure, whether it's on reissues of the postcards or in iPhone apps."

And in that way it can be hoped that Arnold Taylor, Brian Fitzpatrick and the other ghosts of Holmfirth are finally recognised as heroes of classic British comedy.

Top: Ian Wallace with two wall signs featuring classic Bamforth artwork.

Above: Derek Bamforth and his wife Peggy pictured at a Huddersfield exhibition of Bamforth postcards in January 2004.

NEWLYWEDS

In post-war Britain, where the stricture of 'no sex before marriage' was at least ostensibly observed by many courting couples, the wedding night became the subject of countless bawdy jokes.

In the days before widespread foreign travel, honeymooning couples often spent their first night together at a seaside resort. The combination of eager anticipation and performance anxiety provided decades of inspiration to Bamforth artists.

It has been a common criticism of saucy postcards that they typify a less enlightened era of laddish jokes made at the expense of women. In 2007 *The Sunday Express* described Bamforth and their contemporaries as representing a "gentle, albeit sexist, tribute to another age."

Bamforth's cards may have perpetuated all manner of stereotypes in British society, but any sexism was clearly a two-way street. The most casual glance at Bamforth's honeymoon cards reveals that most of them must have been aimed at women, as invariably it is the men who are the butt of the jokes. The illustrations offer flattering portrayals of newlywed girls as nubile young nymphs,

while depicting their withering husbands as diminutive or just weedy in comparison. Bridegrooms are repeatedly lampooned for every type of sexual inadequacy, and it's tempting to wonder how many of these cards were bought by disappointed brides after anti-climactic wedding nights.

In the cards chosen here the young couple's journey typically begins at the church and ends with a sexual misadventure that evening. Brian Fitzpatrick's merciless contribution to page 47 was first published in 1971 and earns iconic status by taking place in Blackpool, the spiritual home of both the dirty weekend and the saucy postcard.

Although still very funny, many of Bamforth's newlywed jokes would have little relevance to younger generations to whom wedlock, let alone chastity, has become entirely optional. By the early 1990s it was estimated that less than one per cent of first sexual intercourse took place within marriage.

But despite that, these cards seem surprisingly modern in at least one respect – in the Bamforth battle of the sexes this round was definitely won by the ladies.

"WHAT ARE YOU DOING YOU FOOL—YOU'RE
SUPPOSED TO PLAY THE WEDDING MARCH
NOT—**RESCUE THE PERISHING!**"

A "BAMFORTH" COMIC

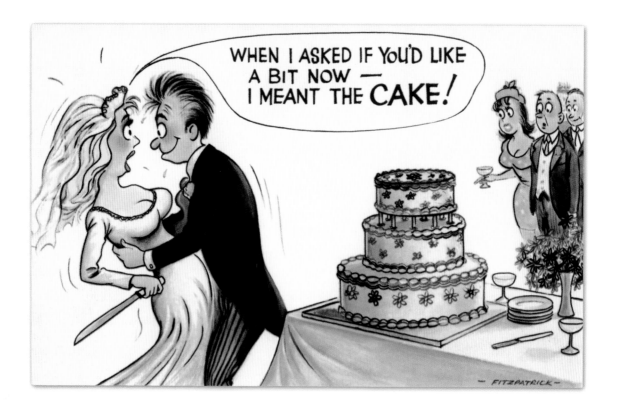

RUDE HEALTH

A nxiety, social embarrassment and a loss of dignity are the catalysts for some of our greatest comedy. So it should come as no surprise that National Health Service hospitals have long been cherished venues for British gag writers.

Medical humour found its biggest audience in 1950s and 60s cinema. *Doctor in the House*, the film adaptation of Richard Gordon's novel, was one of the biggest hits of 1954, leading to six sequels and seven television series. Even better remembered are the *Carry On* team's four excursions into bedpan humour.

The menacing matron in *Carry On Nurse* was the invention of scriptwriter Norman Hudis and actress Hattie Jacques, but many of the other archetypes and situations were already familiar from comic postcards. The following pages feature a ward full of randy patients, incredulous doctors and their medical mishaps. Nearly all the nurses are dolly distractions, of the type personified by the mini-skirted Barbara Windsor in 1967's *Carry On Doctor*. Many of the senior staff are balding middle-aged men dressed in the formal style adopted by the bellowing Sir Lancelot Spratt (James Robertson Justice) in the *Doctor* films.

The cards in this chapter are all set in hospitals, but there are numerous others that mined comedy gold from medical adversity. A 1962 card by Arnold Taylor even mingles toilet humour with a dash of political history. A bedridden Irishman tells a visiting GP: "Sure doctor – my heart's in dear old Ireland!" To which the doctor responds: "Well Murphy, get your bowels in the Free State and you'll be alright!"

Six years later Brian Fitzpatrick found the funny side of tooth decay. A dentist approaches his buxom patient, wielding a drill: "I think I'd rather have a baby than have a tooth filled!" says the nervous girl. "Blimey miss," he replies, "make your mind up before I start!"

The situations depicted in these cards, and perpetuated by the films they helped to inspire, prove that laughter is still the best medicine. The following example from 1974 combines vulgarity and clever wordplay in an outrageous joke that's become a Bamforth classic...

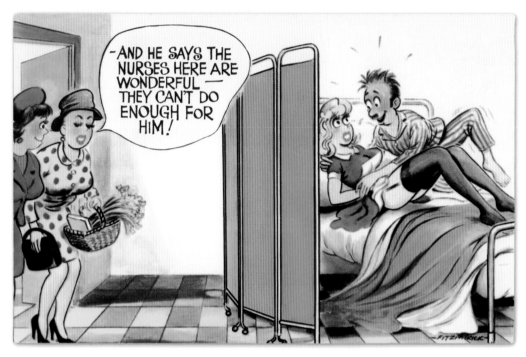

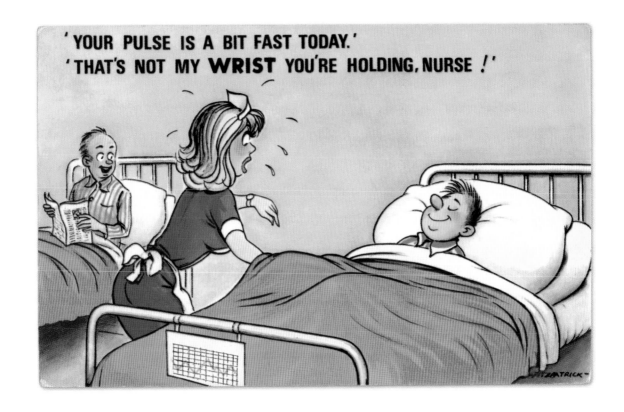

ALL IN A DAY'S WORK

Aside from featuring some of Bamforth's funniest gags, the cards in this chapter serve as a chronicle of changing times: the advent of hire purchase prompts a visit from the debt collector on page 67, and elsewhere deliveries from coal merchants and greengrocers have predictably lewd implications.

The milkman was widely regarded by jealous males as a sexual predator who enlivened his door-to-door duties by servicing his female customers. The comic establishment's over-reliance on milkman gags was satirised in 1969 as part of the first series of *Monty Python's Flying Circus*, but the mistrust of milkmen is still part of our comic DNA. *Speed 3*, a 1998 episode of clerical sitcom *Father Ted*, features grotesque Lothario Pat Mustard (Pat Laffan), a milkman whose round is gladly punctuated by sex-starved housewives.

The Charles Grigg card that appears at the bottom of page 73 is a late entry into our milkmen's hall of fame that proves the gag was alive and well in 1982.

The plumber scenario reproduced twice on page 82 shows how a joke originally published in 1962 could be spruced up for a new generation in 1981. Another perennial is on page 91. A blonde policewoman is arresting a drunk: "Anything you say will be taken down!" she says. "Knickers!" he replies. Of all the 5,000 gags devised by Arnold Taylor for Bamforth, this 1972 card would remain his favourite.

Bamforth weren't above recycling other people's punchlines – the 1970 card on the right of page 76 is a variation on a farming quip immortalised by Charles Hawtrey in the previous year's *Carry On Camping*.

During this era it seems Bamforth were careful not to alienate their working class audience by satirising the trade union movement. The 1970 card on page 88 makes a reference to "pampering the miners", but generally speaking it is human rather than political foibles that are ridiculed here.

The days of coal and greengrocers' deliveries may be over, supplanted by central heating on one hand and home refrigeration on the other. Even the milkman is an increasingly rare sight on our streets. Fortunately Bamforth's light-hearted view of the working day remains timeless.

'MABEL — THE MILKMAN'S BRAGGING THAT HE'S MADE LOVE TO EVERY WOMAN IN THIS STREET EXCEPT ONE!'
'OH — THAT'LL BE THAT SNOOTY WOMAN AT NUMBER TWENTY!!'

84

THE FAMILY WAY

I t is estimated that 70 per cent of all British women have used the contraceptive pill at some stage in their lives, but this is a relatively recent phenomenon. The combined oral contraceptive pill, commonly referred to as 'the birth pill' on Bamforth postcards, was not available from the National Health Service until 1961. Family planning clinics were not officially allowed to prescribe the pill to single women until 1974.

In the post-war years families were bigger, partly as a consequence of poor contraception and the more widely accepted assumption that a woman's place was in the home. Female frustration with this tradition was reflected in Bamforth cards that depict tired-looking mothers trailing a gaggle of unruly children in their wake.

Not all of Bamforth's maternity gags from this era employed the satirical wit sampled here. A cautionary note was sounded by the 1973 card that defined "Trouble" as "household bills... insurance premiums... a wife... and a mistress – all a month overdue!"

A particularly unusual 1972 card from Brian Fitzpatrick featured a simple illustration of a smiling baby in a pram, against a plain red background. "Welcome little stranger, you've made them very glad," began the caption at the top. "You took a big weight off your mother, and made room for your dear old dad!"

This chapter features more than its fair share of ruddy-faced officials, in this case outraged by the pronouncements of naïve young mums-to-be. It's refreshing, however, to see this role taken by a female shop assistant and a fortune teller in the two examples from Bamforth's mid-60s Slim Comic range that appear on page 96.

Another of Fitzpatrick's Slim Comic cards didn't make this selection, partly because it doesn't actually feature a funny illustration. It begins by appearing to advocate the admirable campaign encouraging new mums to breast feed, before descending to the familiar smut: "Mother's milk is best because – it's hygienic... it's germ free... the cat can't get at it... and it comes in attractive containers!"

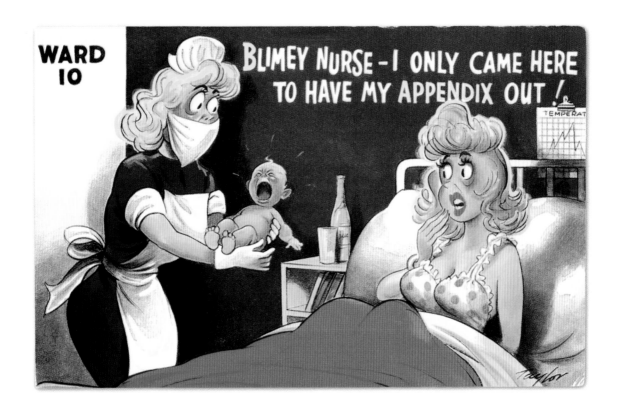

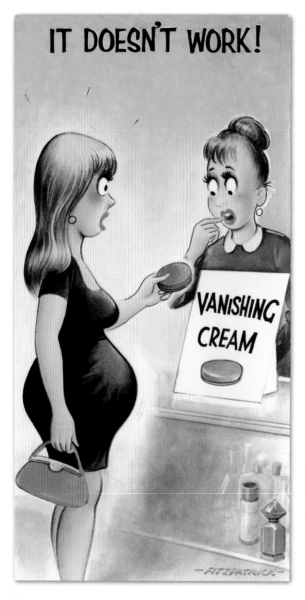

THE DEMON DRINK

Illustrations featuring drunkards had been a staple of the Bamforth catalogue since Douglas Tempest, the company's original artist, established the style of its comic postcards. Between the wars, Tempest was particularly adept at drawing moon-faced, rosy-cheeked inebriates with dishevelled collars and literal cross-eyes. In a familiar routine possibly inspired by Hollywood comedian WC Fields, Tempest's drunks imparted slurred words of wisdom to similarly sloshed companions or, quite often, inanimate objects.

After the war Tempest's rather gentle style gave way to more ribald scenarios that nevertheless retained the affectionate and essentially good-natured humour that characterised Bamforth's output. Crucially there was nothing judgemental about the company's depiction of alcoholism, which was just as well given that many of these jokes would be sold cheek by jowl with Bamforth advertising cards promoting such beverages as Guinness's Extra Stout and Bass Pale Ale.

Some designs merely celebrated the simple joys of drinking. Both Philip and Arnold Taylor contributed to a series that portrayed various jolly figures relishing foaming pints of ale. "Feel okay since I came here, enjoying myself and the beer," declared one beaming holidaymaker. "Pack your blinking bag and come, and I'll be pleased to buy you one!"

By the 1960s there were numerous gags concerning drink driving, many of which would probably be frowned upon today. The Road Safety Act of 1967 introduced a maximum blood alcohol level for drivers, enforced by the use of the breathalyser. This was closely followed by a number of cards from Arnold Taylor and Brian Fitzpatrick, both clearly amused by the idea of police asking drunks to blow into plastic bags.

Never one to miss an opportunity, Fitzpatrick had already found a way to mix a comic cocktail from the generally incompatible ingredients of alcoholism and sex. One of his cards features two drunks staggering down the road. The first is struggling to balance a tray of drinks. "I feel like a ruddy barmaid Fred!" he says. His mate replies, "I do lad – but where can we get one at this time of night?"

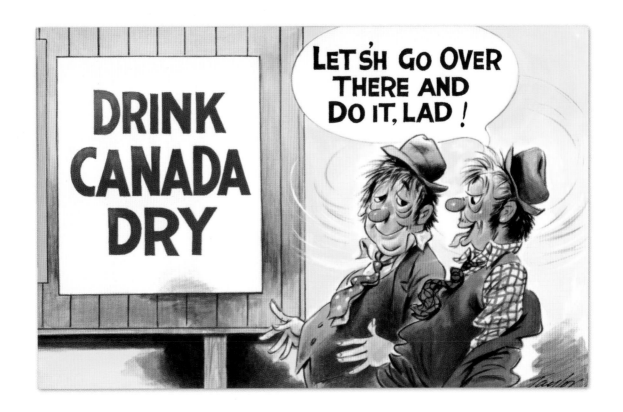

GRIN AND BARE IT

Unlike some of our more relaxed European counterparts, the British have generally remained sceptical about the idea of topless beaches and nudist camps. It's hardly surprising, with a climate that's rarely conducive to the public baring of flesh.

The reputation of British naturists was hardly improved by the earliest films on the subject. Notorious efforts such as *Nudes of the World* (1961) and *Take Off Your Clothes and Live!* (1962) were part of a short-lived trend that exploited censors' loopholes to deliver thinly veiled (albeit distinctly coy) pornography. The sequence in the cinema at the beginning of *Carry On Camping* (1969) tells you all you need to know about such films without the inconvenience of actually having to watch one.

Bamforth had beat the filmmakers to it, publishing cards set in nudist camps as early as the 1930s. Like the film pornographers that succeeded them, Bamforth artists perpetuated the myth that most naturists are fit young men and women. In those days, illustrating bare boobs – let alone bare anything else – was out of the question, so in 1937 Arnold Taylor had to get the point across by showing a beautiful girl peering over the boundary of the 'Ladies' Nudist Club'. "There's a hole in our fence I'd like you to board up!" she tells a passing workman. "Don't worry, Miss," he replies. "I'll look into it!"

A Brian Fitzpatrick card from 1962 shows a blonde camper discreetly covering her top half with a copy of the Club Rules while her male friend cooks breakfast. "I know it's against the rules," he tells her, "but if you think I'm going to fry bacon without an apron – you're ruddy well mistaken!"

Naturism became the longest-running theme for Bamforth's comic series, and by the late 1960s the ladies no longer needed fences or books to hide behind. Despite the fact that an astonishing number of these cards were produced, it could be argued that the subject inspired the narrowest variety of jokes. Obsessions included leering men and women, mismatched pubic hair and genital imperilment by everything from stray geese to lawnmowers. Prepare to wince...

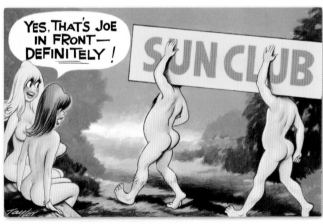

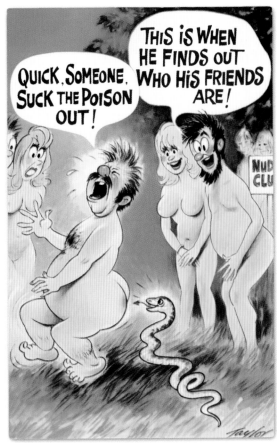

WEDDED BLISS

After the honeymoon, the hangover. Published in an era when divorce was more difficult, and less socially acceptable, Bamforth's comic cards are full of squabbling couples, repenting at leisure while they endure snoring, flagging libidos and general neglect. The chilling consequences of monogamy are made clear in numerous cards that feature brow-beaten husbands harangued by their stout and sexually frustrated wives.

This chapter features the obligatory mother-in-law gag and three rare excursions into medieval history, including a cameo from a long-haired Robin Hood. For the most part, however, these depictions of marital strife take place against a contemporary backdrop of the Green Shield Stamps loyalty scheme, electric organs (no sniggering at the back) and supermarket shopping. In the early 1970s' cards there are references to the energy crisis and the 'Clunk Click Every Trip' road safety slogan, encouraging drivers to wear seat belts in an era before it was compulsory by law.

A popular series of cards, launched in 1944 and refreshed over the decades, offered advice on 'How to treat the wife' and 'How to treat the husband'. Bamforth's marriage guidance included the following tips for the gentlemen: "Do everything you can for her, and if that doesn't satisfy her, ask her if there's anything else she wants, and whatever it is she wants, let her have it, and if that doesn't satisfy her, DROWN HER!" The message for the ladies began: "Always give him a kiss when you go out and when you come in. Always give him back what you save of your housekeeping money. Always let him have the best chair (if you've only one chair, you stand up)..." before concluding that if he still isn't happy then "SHOOT THE DEVIL!"

For all the cynicism surrounding marriage, one of Bamforth's most memorable designs portrayed the longing for an absent partner. This 1944 card by Arnold Taylor depicted a forlorn young woman, alone in bed. On the wall is a picture of her husband in soldier's uniform. "I do miss my hubby," she says. "No cup o' tea, no nothing!"

GOOD SPORTS

ocker rooms, odd-shaped balls and fishermen's friends were all grist to the comic mill for Bamforth artists, but some of the best sporting-themed innuendo came from less obvious subjects.

The traditionally male pursuits of weight-lifting and football are celebrated on page 155. Both are relatively rare forays into these territories, and it's puzzling that football in particular is not better represented in Bamforth's comic series.

Surprisingly, given the company's traditional working class constituency, golf remained a popular theme for decades. Quite how so many naked women came to recline in the long grass on golf courses is never adequately explained, unless the courses in question neighbour nudist camps.

The first illustration in this chapter is by the uncredited Arnold Taylor and is the best of several variations on the improbable scenario that a figure skater would somehow lose her knickers. Although the predicament in 1965's "Hey Sonia!" was entirely fictional, the girl in the picture was probably inspired by Sonja Henie. The Norwegian figure skater was an Olympic champion in 1928, 1932 and 1936, and the first to compete wearing a short skirt. When her competitive career was over she fulfilled a long-held ambition to become a film star, becoming one of the highest paid actresses in Hollywood.

Taylor's original artwork for "Hey Sonia!" was among numerous items from the Bamforth archive sold by London auction house Christie's on 17 February 1994. "Hey Sonia!" was in the same lot as ten other pieces by Taylor and Charles Griggs, with an estimate of £150-250. The following day *The Financial Times* reported that the lot had sold for £3,850, a record price for any postcard artwork. The lucky bidder was a New York-based British collector. He had been particularly keen to purchase "Hey Sonia!" because he had once sent the corresponding postcard to the legendary pop artist Andy Warhol.

After the sale the unnamed collector told *The Independent*, "In my view, 'Hey Sonia!' is just as important as the Mona Lisa in that it is so widely circulated in workmen's huts and schoolboys' lockers, and seen all over the world."

'BLIMEY MATE FOR TWENTY FIVE BOB I CAN GET A **WOMAN**!'
'AYE SON, BUT YOU CAN'T GET FORTY FIVE MINUTES EACH WAY, AND A BRASS BAND THROWN IN AT HALF-TIME!'

GETTING THE PICTURE

This chapter features some of Bamforth's most inventive comic postcards – designs that primarily rely on a picture, rather than a written gag, to raise a laugh.

The "Hey Sonia!" tradition of sportswomen losing their knickers was continued in an Arnold Taylor card that shows a blonde high-diver who is heading towards the water when she discovers the lower half of her bikini is round her ankles. Taylor returned to the scene of his figure-skating triumph with the amusing but improbable scenario that appears on page 171.

Taylor was also a prolific contributor to what can best be described as the "Bloody hell!" school of sight gags – these portray an unsuspecting victim of a mishap that occurs in the underwear department. Or at least it would if they were wearing any. There are several cards that show naked swimmers menaced by sharp-toothed sea life – a 1974 example involving a vulnerable male swimmer and a hungry-looking crocodile lends this sub-genre its name. Five years later another "Bloody hell!" was exclaimed by a snooker referee who is standing right behind a player and catches the wrong end of his cue as a result. The most unsubtle of Taylor's cards employs the rather less controversial exclamation "Ow!!" but shows a naked man suddenly trapped between the jaws of a toilet and its collapsing lid.

Brian Fitzpatrick was similarly keen on purely visual jokes – his pantomime horse on page 166 is one of the outstanding examples here. Note how even the horse is laughing. Some of Fitzpatrick's favourite sight gags involved sculptors – in one, the artist in question makes a slip and changes the name of his subject from 'Bert' to 'Bertha'. He was also fond of showing trapeze artists, pictured at the embarrassing moment where they grabbed onto something inappropriate.

As proof that a picture paints a thousand words, here are some of the cleverest jokes in the whole series (the staircase encounter on page 171) alongside some of the most abstract (the card at the top of page 169 must be one of the strangest Bamforth ever published) and, in the case of page 168, one of the downright naughtiest.

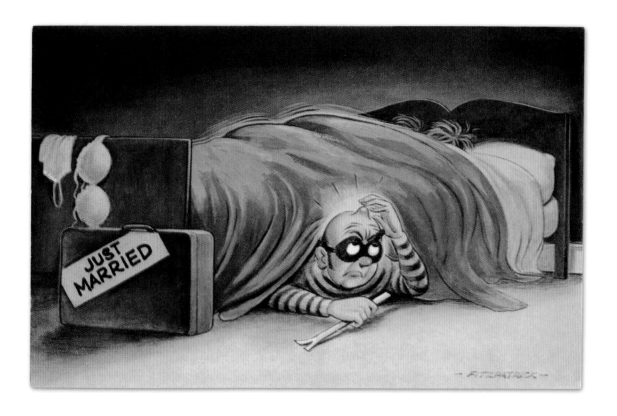

THE GOGGLE BOX

Television had a huge impact on cinema attendance in the post-war years. Bamforth's artists clearly recalled the courting rituals in the back rows of their local fleapits but, like many of the customers for their postcards, eventually settled for a quiet night in front of the box. Or not so quiet, according to some of the distracted viewers depicted here.

The first card in this chapter makes reference to the 'X' certificate, a notorious classification upheld by the British Board of Film Censors. This was an 'adults only' category, which from 1951 to 1970 restricted viewing by anyone under the age of 16. Originally designed to categorise sex films imported from the Continent, the X became better known for its association with horror movies and retained its forbidden connotations long after it was abolished in 1982.

Censorship wasn't confined to films. In 1953, the year television came of age with the Queen's coronation, Arnold Taylor advocated discretion in a card showing a portly couple undressing. "By gum," says the husband, "I hope you never get *us* on television round about bed time!" Nine years later self-appointed moral guardian Mary Whitehouse launched the rather more serious 'Clean Up TV Campaign'. Her concerns are shared by the disrobing wife on page 191.

There are many other highlights for social and cultural historians in this selection of cards. Aside from the illustrations featuring outside lavatories, there are mentions of long-gone television shows such as the voyeuristic *Candid Camera*, daytime soap *Crossroads*, the BBC's *Sportsview* and ITV's Saturday afternoon wrestling. The slick TV presenter on page 189 would have been familiar as the host of a long-running series of commercials asking shoppers if they could tell the difference between Stork margarine and butter. The ubiquitous ads weren't just parodied by Bamforth – in 1969 *Monty Python's Flying Circus* reported that "nine out of ten housewives can't tell the difference between Whizzo Butter and a dead crab."

The sheer novelty of television must account for the preponderance of cards that now seem rather quaint in an age where even the most sophisticated set is just part of the furniture.

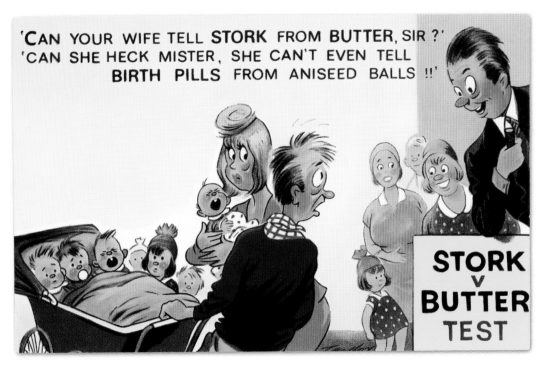

THE PERMISSIVE SOCIETY

Along with sea and sand, a bit of slap and tickle has long been considered an essential component of the British holiday experience. This was acknowledged by Bamforth on even the tamest seaside postcards issued by the company after the war.

Arnold Taylor had a charming line in canoodling couples during this era. One of his designs features a girl in a polka dot swimsuit, posing with a gentleman friend on the beach. "Getting just what the doctor ordered," she tells the folks back home. "Having a marvellous time!"

Another card features a couple cuddling on a pier. "Don't care if it snows – having a great time! (There are plenty of cosy corners here!)" A 1947 illustration from Taylor shows a girl sitting across her boyfriend's knee. The censorship committees were doubtless appeased by the accompanying caption: "On the last lap, but having a marvellous time," she says. "Don't worry, I haven't forgotten mother's good advice."

The progressive liberalisation of Britain's youth can be traced through the cards in Bamforth's archive. In 1952 the girl remembering mother's good advice gave way to the blonde bombshell who is interrupted while cuddling her boyfriend on the living room sofa. Mother: "Well!! – I never did!!" Daughter: "Don't be daft mother – you must have done!"

By the late 1960s there were fewer coy lovers on park benches and rather more references to randy students, the hippy movement and the impracticalities of getting your leg over in a Mini. One card from 1973 included a poem about that very problem: "They tried it on the sofa, They tried it in the bath, They tried it in the park – even on the path, But wherever they tried it... The least success by far, was when they tried to do it... in a Mini car!"

As the influence of the censorship committees receded, the artists at Bamforth adopted a more relaxed attitude towards taboo subjects. Jokes would become increasingly explicit until innuendo – the fine art that once defined the saucy postcard – seemed redundant.

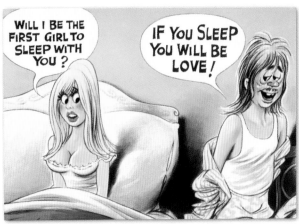

THE MODERN WORLD

Times were changing. Men's hair was getting longer and girl's skirts were getting shorter. Young people were enjoying unprecedented disposable income and a new sexual liberation – much to the consternation of their parents and the artists at the Bamforth studio.

The hubs of the new revolution were record shops, and these made several appearances on Bamforth cards. Numerous early 1960s groups were namechecked, although Taylor and Fitzpatrick's misspelling of Cliff Richard's surname shows that they weren't quite as groovy as the ravers on page 213.

The rather lame farmyard gag at the bottom of page 214 references the radio show *Pick of the Pops*, which ran in its original format from 1955 to 1972, and elsewhere the portable wireless is shown as the essential accessory for the 'with it' teenager.

In 1966, two years after rioting mods and rockers tore up British seaside towns, intimidated retailers could get their revenge with the card reproduced on page 222. Making the more menacing rockers the butt of a similar joke was presumably considered too risky.

It was no longer possible to tell the difference between the sexes, and even currency was changing. The reluctant young lady on page 220 is declining to accept a new method of payment launched in 1972. The Access card's reputation as 'your flexible friend' seems rather at odds with the aims of its eager owner.

It could be argued that Taylor and Fitzpatrick's satirical view of the 'in crowd' was a reactionary watershed. A publisher that once represented the counter-culture, a victim of censorship committees and an obscenity trial, was now aligned to an establishment bemused by the younger generation's freedom of expression.

Bamforth continued to publish new and reissued designs for over 30 years after the sexual revolution, but from the 1970s onwards the cards would increasingly be perceived as a quaint reminder of Britain's sexual austerity.

The relative absence of such innocent naughtiness in the modern world has provided the best of these cards with a continued life. And allowed what once seemed transgressive to be reclaimed as nostalgia.

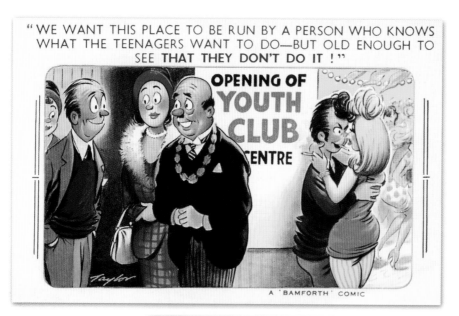

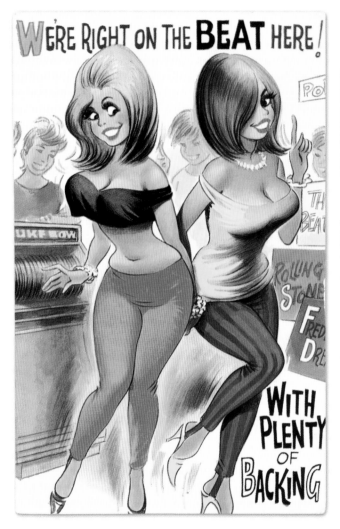

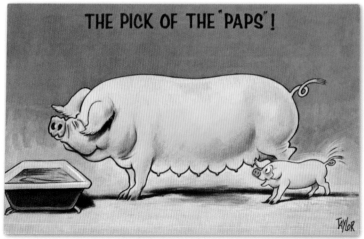

ABOUT THE AUTHOR

Since beginning his career at Marvel Comics in 1993, Marcus Hearn has written for *The Times*, *The Guardian* and *The Independent*, as well as contributing booklet notes, audio commentaries and documentaries to nearly 100 DVDs. His numerous books include authorised biographies of filmmakers George Lucas and Gerry Anderson, *The Avengers: A Celebration* and *Eight Days a Week*, the story of The Beatles' final world tour. He is an associate research fellow at Leicester de Montfort's Cinema and Television History Research Centre, and is the official historian of Hammer Film Productions.

ACKNOWLEDGEMENTS

Special thanks to Bernard Crossley for his valuable comments on the manuscript, and his willingness to share information and original artwork from his remarkable collection. Dr Nick Hiley's insights into the censorship of comic postcards were similarly helpful.

At Bamforth & Co, my thanks to Ian Wallace, David Dawson, Amy Allison and especially my old friend Janet Woodward. Charlie Mounter is my new favourite editor, and it's always a pleasure to work with designer Peri Godbold and picture researcher David Pratt.

My thanks also to Sharon Ankin, Alan Barnes, Jo Botting, David Dickens, Jonathan Rigby, Jack Sammons, Lyn Shields, Paul Taylor, Peter Tucker, Jo Ware and Gary Worsnop.

The British Cartoon Archive, The British Film Institute, Lucerna – the Magic Lantern Web Resource and The Yorkshire Film Archive were useful sources of information, as were:

Bamforth & Co by Ralph Jones (unpublished manuscript, 1964)
Bound and Gagged: A Secret History of Obscenity in Britain by Alan Travis (Profile, 2000)
The Comic Postcard in English Life by Frederick Alderson (David & Charles, 1970)
Picture Postcard Monthly (edited by Brian Lund)

All images in this book are © Bamforth & Co Ltd, with the following exceptions:
James Bamforth (page 8), Edwin Bamforth (page 10) and Derek Bamforth (page 28) © June Couch
Douglas and Margaret Tempest (page 12) © Rebecca Addis
The Brook (page 16) © Brook Electric Motors Ltd
Arnold Taylor and Brian Fitzpatrick (page 17) © *The Huddersfield Daily Examiner*
Christie's catalogue (page 28) © Christie's South Kensington Ltd
Ian Wallace (page 29) © Roy Hampson
Derek and Peggy Bamforth (page 29) © Bernard Crossley